Praise for The Torch Corri

"What a joyful recommendation I have for parents! There could be no more beautiful biography on the life of Corrie ten Boom for children than this one. It is very well and accurately written with a wonderful array of pictures to keep the book appealing and interesting. This is a true biography, not historical fiction, and will fill a void for an age group that has few well-written biographies about people of faith.

And it delights me more than anything else that this biography ends with the message which Corrie ten Boom spent decades seeking to highlight above all else: Forgiveness of our enemies through the power of the Holy Spirit. A vital message for our children."

Pam Rosewell Moore, *former personal assistant to Corrie ten Boom, author, and speaker*

"As a child, I learned forgiveness from Corrie Ten Boom's story. Years later I would need to practice that very thing when we were held hostage in the jungle. I am grateful for her example and life!!"

Gracia Burnham, *New Tribes Mission, author*

"Kids will love this riveting story! Congrats to Christian History Institute for a tale well told."

Meg Moss, *contributing editor of* Ask, *"Arts and Sciences for Kids," magazine*

"Intermediate grade students want facts. They also want heroes. This book delivers on both, and it does so in the most readable and engaging way. I so look forward to sharing this high-quality Christian biography with my students."

Sharon Reynolds, *M.Ed.,Certified Reading Specialist (K–12)*

"*Corrie ten Boom* tells a powerful story of a family's love, sacrifice, and obedience to God. Torchlighters resources are a wonderful way to introduce children to testimonies of God's faithfulness in times of persecution and to the perseverance and courage of bold Christians who serve Him in difficult times and places."

Jim Dau, *President and CEO, The Voice of the Martyrs; father of three, grandfather of ten*

Corrie ten Boom

A Biography

Kaylena Radcliff

The Torchlighters Biography Series: Corrie ten Boom
by Kaylena Radcliff

Published by

The Christian History Institute, Pennsylvania, USA
Herald Entertainment, Inc., USA

Editor: Dawn Moore
Editorial Advisor: Frits Nieuwstraten
Editorial Assistant: Robin Woodall
Creative Director: Robert Fernandez
Design & Layout: Gamaliel Erlan, Robert Fernandez
Cover & Illustrations: Herald Entertainment, Inc., with stills from the
animated film, *The Torchlighters: The Corrie ten Boom Story*

Photographs provided by the Corrie ten Boom Museum,
www.corrietenboom.com.

Printed in the United States of America
First printing 2014

ISBN 978-1 56364 873 1

Table of contents

ICELAND

FINLAN

NORWAY

SWEDEN

ES

DENMARK

LITH

IRELAND

GREAT
BRITAIN

NETHERLANDS

POLAND

GERMANY

BELGIUM

LUX.

CZECH
REPUBLIC

SLOVAKIA

FRANCE

AUSTRIA

HUNGARY

SWITZERLAND

SLOVENIA

CROATIA

ITALY

BOSNIA
& HER

YUGO

SPAIN

ALBAN

8

Interesting Facts about the Netherlands!

Its official name is the Netherlands, but most people refer to it as "Holland." North Holland and South Holland are two large provinces in the Netherlands. The biggest cities in the country are located there.

Whether you call it the Netherlands or Holland, the people there are known as the Dutch, and their official language is also Dutch.

Tulips did not originate in Holland, but became popular there in the early 1600s. The Dutch climate is perfectly suited to the beautiful flowers, and the Netherlands is now the world's biggest exporter of tulip bulbs.

Orange is the official color of the Netherlands, in honor of the royal family, the House of Orange.

Wooden shoes, or clogs, were first worn over 800 years ago. Some farmers still wear them because they are good for walking on muddy soil and are easy to put on and off.

There are over 1,000 windmills in the Netherlands.

Chapter

1

∼ Corrie and the Red Cap Club ∼

The smell of spring was in the air as a young woman with brown hair led a group of seven bubbling children along the streets of Haarlem, a city in the country of **Holland**. It was 1925. The woman, named Cornelia ten Boom, glanced over her shoulder to make sure the children kept up. Though unmarried at the age of thirty-three, Corrie could not help but feel like a mother to these children. They bounced along eagerly behind her, laughing and playing as they went. And they all held tightly to bright red caps on their heads.

"Well!" said the streetcar conductor as the group passed. "Here comes Corrie ten Boom and her Red Cap Club!"

Corrie waved and smiled politely at the man. *Oh, those red caps!* she thought. The red hats were a gift from one of Corrie's business associates. Ever since they arrived, the children would not stop wearing them. It sure did make them look like a club whenever they went out!

As the children bobbed happily behind her, Corrie led them back to the **Beje** (bay-yay). This was the nickname for the warm and loving home of the Ten Boom family. It was an old, funny-looking house—tall, crooked, and sandwiched tightly between the buildings on the crowded street. It was the home Corrie grew up in and a place full of happy memories.

Father ten Boom, whom the children called Opa (which means grandfather), was waiting for them. He was fixing watches in his shop downstairs. Betsie, one of Corrie's older sisters, was busy cooking up a nutritious meal for everyone.

Corrie sighed with contentment, glad to know that God could use what little they had to help these children.

Corrie's beloved home—the Beje.

Casper ten Boom busy in his watch shop.

It's so nice to hear the sound of laughter ringing through the house again! Corrie thought. She marveled at how things had changed since her own childhood. Two of her older siblings, brother Willem and sister Nollie, had married and moved away. Corrie's three aunts, who had lived with them in the Beje since she was little, had all passed away over these last few years. Even Mama, whom Corrie loved very much, was now in heaven. Now it was only Father, Corrie, and Betsie in the Beje. Well, them, and the Red Cap Club!

Corrie smiled as she thought of how her family had taught her to trust in Jesus. She was sure Mama was smiling from heaven now too as Corrie led the group into the old house. It was Mama, after all, who told Corrie that God could use her special gifts to help children.

"God has big plans for you, Corrie!" Mama had said years before. "If you want to serve God by teaching children, it would be a great thing." While Corrie agreed with Mama, she did not see how she could do it. As a watchmaker in Father's shop, she was so busy! Even so, she felt God's tug on her heart to do something more. Then, God showed her what He wanted her to do.

It all started with Puck, Hans, and Hardy. Since their parents were missionaries very far away, they needed a place to go. Father, Betsie, and Corrie all agreed to take them in. Soon, the old house was filled to the brim with children! Corrie was glad. These children needed a home, and now they lived happily in the Beje. And just like Mama had said, Corrie taught them about Jesus.

Sometimes Corrie worried about having enough money and food to keep them there, but God always provided. In fact, it always seemed there was room for one more smiling face. Now, seven foster children lived with the Ten Booms.

These seven children were Corrie's Red Cap Club. When they got back to the Beje, the smell of something delicious wafted out from the open windows. Corrie smiled as the children ran in ahead of her, excited to see Opa and Tante (aunt) Betsie.

In this happy moment, Corrie thought about what the future might hold. What would it bring? She could not know that years later, when these children were grown and married, the Ten Booms would foster a new kind of family. She could not know that her God, who was doing big things right now, had even bigger things in store.

Corrie (left) and Betsie (front), along with their father and children of missionaries.

Chapter

2

❧ A Distant Rumble ❧

Corrie hurried through the Beje, careful not to catch the hem of her new dress on doors and corners as she sped down the stairs. It was still very early on this cold January morning in 1937, twelve years since the Red Cap Club roamed the halls of the old house. The floorboards creaked as Corrie thumped down the stairs, reminding her of how quiet the Beje had become since the children grew up and left the home.

Well! Corrie thought. *It won't be quiet today!* The doorbell was already buzzing, and for good reason. Today was the one-hundredth-birthday party of the Ten Boom Watch Shop, started years ago by Corrie's grandfather. Corrie rounded the corner to find Betsie ahead at the door, letting in the first of the guests to arrive. Corrie smiled as she thought of her mother. How Mama would have loved today's party!

Betsie bustled around to make order of the quickly filling house. Even still, she had a wide smile on her face and a playful spring in her step. As the flowers came in, Betsie was quick to arrange them and place them around the home.

"Oh Corrie! Just look how these brighten up everything!"

"Oh, yes! They look just perfect!" Corrie agreed. She smiled at Betsie before hurrying off to set the breakfast table. Father would be awake soon, and she wanted to make sure everything was ready.

At 8:10, Father Casper ten Boom came down to the dining room, just as he always did. His hair and beard were both as white as snow, but his blue eyes still twinkled like a child's as he looked over the bright, crowded room.

"How happy and lovely you both look!" he said, hugging his two daughters tightly.

Though the old house was busy and bustling with guests, Father sat everyone down to say the blessing for breakfast as usual. He also pulled his old Bible off the shelf, and, just like every morning, he read loudly and thoughtfully from God's word. For Father, this is how each and every day should start, even on one-hundredth birthdays.

It seemed everyone in the city came to congratulate Father and the family on this big day. Friends, neighbors, policemen, and even the mayor came to visit! Corrie's sister Nollie also arrived with her children, all of them tidy and well dressed for the special occasion. Peter, one of Corrie's nephews, gave her a quick hug before sitting at the old piano to show off his musical talent. Corrie shook her head, but could not help grinning. Peter's music brightened every party.

Father ten Boom (front and center) and his guests.

Corrie counted heads as guests flooded the house. She frowned. *Where was Willem?* Corrie poked her head outside and searched the empty street for her missing brother. Disappointed, Corrie came back inside. She sat at the small kitchen table, where the guests talked in hushed tones about something that scared her: rumors of war.

Something bad was happening in Germany, the country next to Holland. Businesses were closing, and people were trying to leave the country. Would there be war? Corrie listened, the worry in their voices creeping into her own heart. Germany had not fought with Holland during the last war, but it sounded to Corrie like these new stirrings were different. Whatever was brewing in Germany was sure to boil over into Holland.

Suddenly, Willem burst into the room with his wife and four children in tow. A ragged man leaned on Willem's side. The man wore a broad-brimmed black hat and a tattered, long coat. Corrie could tell from these clothes that the man was a Jew. He looked battered and tired. Corrie gasped as she caught sight of his face. Where his long, full beard should have been, there were deep burns and raw, bloody patches of skin instead.

"This is Mr. Gutlieber," Willem said, introducing him to Father and the family. In a low voice, Willem quickly told them what happened. Mr. Gutlieber was trying to leave Germany, but before he could get out, a few boys attacked him and set his beard on fire. Corrie cringed in horror. Why would someone want to hurt him? She remembered how the Bible said that the Jews were God's chosen people. As a Christian, Corrie tried to treat all people with kindness. Did not God's people deserve kindness too? Compassion filled her heart as she looked at their new guest's burned face. She did her best to make him comfortable.

As talk around the table started up again, Corrie could not shake the chill that settled in her bones. Even on this happy day, Corrie could hear it—the distant rumble of things to come. Corrie held the cup of coffee in her lap tightly and tried to ignore the feeling. She quietly watched as rolling storm clouds gathered just outside the kitchen window, slowly but surely darkening the January sky.

Somehow, she knew an even bigger storm was headed their way.

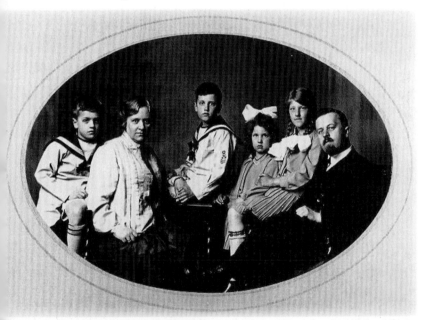

Corrie's brother, Willem, and his family.

Chapter

3

∾ **There Will Be War** ∾

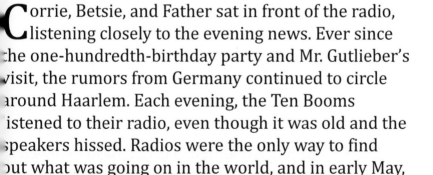

Corrie, Betsie, and Father sat in front of the radio, listening closely to the evening news. Ever since the one-hundredth-birthday party and Mr. Gutlieber's visit, the rumors from Germany continued to circle around Haarlem. Each evening, the Ten Booms listened to their radio, even though it was old and the speakers hissed. Radios were the only way to find out what was going on in the world, and in early May, 1940, there was a lot to hear.

Corrie's country, Holland, was in danger of being attacked. The Germans, led by **Adolf Hitler**, were sweeping across Europe and taking over many countries close to Holland. Corrie fidgeted nervously as the broadcast came over the radio. *Was Holland* *next?* Soon, the prime minister's voice crackled through the speaker.

"Germany will not attack us," he promised. "There is nothing to be afraid of."

At this announcement, Father angrily switched off the radio.

"The prime minister is a fool!" Father said. "The Germans will come, and we will fall. God help everyone who does not call on the name of the Lord!"

Corrie stared at Father in shock as he turned sharply and went up the stairs to bed. Normally, Father was very peaceful and gentle! To say such a thing about the prime minister, an important leader of Holland, was unlike him. Corrie and Betsie looked at each other in stunned disbelief. But somehow, they knew he was right. Finally, Corrie and Betsie followed Father up to bed, an uneasy feeling fluttering in their bellies.

BOOM! Corrie sat up suddenly in bed, startled. *What was that?* She wondered. A bright flash followed by a loud boom erupted in the quiet night. As her bed shook, Corrie crawled quickly toward her window and peered outside. The sky glowed scarlet as bombs exploded on the ground just outside of her city of Haarlem.

Throwing on her bathrobe, Corrie hurried down the stairs to her sister's room. Betsie was awake, sitting up in her own bed. The Beje shook as more bombs fell.

"War!" they cried as they held each other in the dark.

The whole city quaked and skies flashed. *Was this really happening?* Corrie thought, frightened. *What will become of our country if the Germans bring their hatred here? What will happen to Holland?*

As these questions rolled around in her head, Corrie wondered if she was strong enough to trust in her God, even now.

"Corrie!" Betsie said, shaking Corrie from her thoughts. "Let's go downstairs to pray."

"Oh, yes," Corrie agreed, and she followed Betsie to the kitchen.

Betsie grabbed Corrie's hand as they knelt down to pray. Corrie prayed for all those she could think of, including Queen Wilhelmina and the prime minister. When Corrie finished, Betsie kept praying in a gentle, calm voice.

"God," she said, "we pray for those German pilots in the planes right now. They're also stuck in this great evil of hatred and violence. Please open their eyes to it and bless them."

Corrie's eyes snapped open. She stared at Betsie, shocked. *How could she pray for those evil people?* But Betsie prayed on. Corrie could tell that Betsie believed God's grace was for everyone—even those who carried out Hitler's awful plans.

"Oh Lord," Corrie said as she closed her eyes

once more. "Listen to Betsie, not me. I can't pray for those men in the planes at all."

All of a sudden, a vision formed in Corrie's mind—one so vivid and real that it seemed she was really there. Corrie saw herself, her father, Betsie, and many others she knew. A large wagon that they could not leave was taking them away. It took them far away from Haarlem into a new and terrifying world.

Corrie shivered. Was this thought nothing? Or could it be a vision of what was to come? As she knelt there, praying, Corrie could not be sure about the future, but she did know this: her world was about to change forever.

For the next five days, everyone in Holland held their breath as their **Dutch** soldiers fought against the Germans. The Ten Booms kept the shop open—not to sell watches, but so that people could talk with Father. Many came to the shop and prayed with Father for their husbands and sons out fighting. Corrie brought the radio down from the house and set it atop the display case in the shop. It hummed constantly with news about the war. Most of the news was not good.

Soon, the radio brought news that the queen had left Holland. Corrie, Betsie, and Father walked outside in disbelief. *If the queen has left, what hope do we have?* Everyone else was out in the streets too. On that morning of May 14, 1940, they knew that the end was coming soon.

Above them, a window flew open, and a man leaned out.

"We've surrendered!" he cried.

Corrie clasped Betsie's hand tightly in hers as the bad news rang in her ears.

Holland had fallen.

The newspaper reports the surrender of Holland.

Chapter

4

❦ The Jewish Problem ❦

Corrie leaned in close to her old, heavy radio as it crackled to life.

"Yes, the Germans continue to be victorious," a voice said through the static. "But have courage, my fellow Dutchmen. Help is on the way."

Corrie held her breath to listen, not daring to turn the radio's volume up. In the other room, Betsie banged loudly on the piano to drown out the radio. Though the Free Dutch broadcast was illegal, it was the only way for the Ten Booms to get news from the outside world. Corrie looked around nervously as the broadcast continued. Would the sounds of the piano be enough to drown out the crackle of the radio?

It was 1941, a year after the invasion, and Germany now ruled Holland with cruel force. The German occupation had not started this way, of course. At first, the rules didn't seem too bad. The soldiers made the people of Haarlem follow a curfew. This meant everyone had to be inside before a certain time every night. If anyone was caught in the streets after curfew, that person could be taken to jail. But soon, the German rules became more unfair.

The soldiers told everyone they had to carry an identity card with special markings. They also made the people use ration cards to buy food and other things they needed. The only way to eat and buy supplies was to use the ration cards from the German soldiers. It was hard to live this way. Corrie hated how the Germans controlled everything, but she thanked God that the Germans were not hurting people as long as they followed the rules.

But as time went by, the German rules became even more harsh. Now, they banned every house radio. They only allowed German newspapers and stories, which gave only the German side of the news. Corrie hid her family's old radio so that they could still get news of what was really happening outside of Holland. Doing such a thing was very dangerous.

Worry crept into Corrie's mind as she listened to the Free Dutch broadcast. *I could be sent to jail if the Germans ever found out!* She turned up the radio slightly. To her dismay, the news of the outside world was always grim. The Germans were attacking many other nations, and they were winning. Now, they wanted to take over England, one of the last safe places in Europe. Scared, Corrie prayed for an end to the war. *Lord, please send someone to stop the Germans soon.*

But Corrie's loss of freedom under the occupation was not the worst thing about the Germans' war. It was the ideas of the German leader, Adolf Hitler, and his **Nazi** party that troubled Corrie more than anything else. These Nazi Germans believed that they were the "pure" race. They thought that people with white skin and good health were the best and everyone else was weak and worthless.

Nazi soldiers round up Jews.

Many people in Holland fit into the Nazis' idea of a "pure" race. But the Jewish people did not. In Germany, Hitler blamed the Jews for all of their country's troubles. Now, the Germans wanted to convince everyone that the Jews were the problem for Holland too—a problem that they should get rid of. To Corrie's horror, as the Germans stayed longer in her country, their message of hatred toward Jews began to spread. Many of her neighbors began to believe the same thing. *How*, Corrie wondered, *could people believe this message of hatred toward the Jews? God's chosen people?*

A Dutch group called the **National Socialist Bond**, or NSB, started to support the Nazis and their ideas about Jews. The NSB became more powerful as many people in Holland decided to join them. Some joined for the extra benefits of more food, better jobs, and bigger houses, but many joined because they believed the Nazis were right.

Each day, as Corrie and Father took their daily walk around the city, Corrie was sad to see how the sickness of the Nazis' hatred spread. The Germans and the NSB were cruel. It did not matter that Corrie's Jewish neighbors were Dutch citizens.

Yellow star patch forced upon all Jews.

They were treated like animals. For example, a Jewish men, women, and children had to wear yellow, six-pointed star on their clothes. Each star had the word *Jood* (Jew) written in black ink at the center. With this visible reminder, the Jews were an easy target for all who agreed with the German Nazi way of thinking.

Signs soon began popping up in shop windows: JEWS WILL NOT BE SERVED. Parks, libraries, restaurants, and theaters all echoed the same tune with a "No Jews" policy. *Where were the Jews supposed to go?* Corrie shook her head in anger and sadness. These places where she had often gone as a girl were now dark reminders of the evil changes in her city.

Then, the Jews began to disappear without a trace. Corrie never knew whether the **Gestapo** took them, or if they escaped Holland for somewhere safer. Corrie was so worried for them. Every day, she prayed with all her might that God would protect His chosen people.

Now, as Corrie and Father arrived at the market, Corrie saw an awful scene unfold. In front of her, the Nazi soldiers surrounded the marketplace, blocking them from going inside. A pale-faced Corrie clutched her chest weakly as she realized what the soldiers were doing. They shoved men, women, and children into the back of a waiting truck. As the truck rumbled to life, Corrie saw that all of the Germans' prisoners wore the yellow star. *Oh Lord!* Corrie thought. *How could this happen?*

Anxious and scared faces of Jewish men, women, and children looked out at her as they huddled in the back of the vehicle. Their yellow stars seemed to blaze against the drab gray of the cloudy sky.

"Those poor people!" Corrie whispered, watching helplessly as the truck sped away. Her heart sank as she thought of their fates. How she wanted to do something! But what? Helping Jews was just as much of a crime as being a Jew. Besides, Corrie reasoned, she was just a poor, middle-aged woman. How could she save the Jews from the enemy's hands?

Maybe she was not able, but her Savior certainly was. Corrie bowed her head as she realized what she must try to do. Mumbling a quick prayer for strength, she hurried home. No matter the risk or the cost, Corrie knew it was time for action.

Chapter

5

❧ Safe Haven ❧

A timid knock rattled the Beje's alley-side door on a mild May night in 1942. Corrie, who was sitting with Father and Betsie in their dining room, glanced out the window. She was surprised to see a heavily clothed woman holding a suitcase standing there. She hurried down to the door and opened it.

"May I come in?" the woman asked in a shaky voice.

"Of course," Corrie replied warmly, stepping aside. Her heart swelled with compassion as she watched the woman shuffle quickly through the door. Her face was pale, and her whole body shook with fear. After meeting Father and Betsie, the woman told them her story.

"My name is Mrs. Kleermaker. I'm a Jew and a shopkeeper," she explained. "The police arrested my husband. My son went into hiding. Yesterday, the police came and told me I had to close my store! I am too afraid to go back, and I heard that you helped a man on the street before. A Jew like me."

This was true. After Corrie decided to do something to help, she and her family took in Jews and hid them from the Germans. Then they would get the Jews to an even safer place out of the city and in the countryside. In this way, the Ten Booms could keep as many Jews in Haarlem as possible from being taken by the soldiers. Father smiled at Mrs. Kleermaker and offered a polite bow.

"God's people are *always* welcome here," said Father

"Yes!" added Betsie enthusiastically. "We have plenty of room. We're so glad to have you!"

Mrs. Kleermaker sniffled as tears of relief trickled down her cheek. Betsie placed a comforting hand on her shoulder and showed her where she could sleep.

Over the next few weeks, a steady stream of desperate Jews just like Mrs. Kleermaker came to the Ten Booms for help. Each day brought new faces to the door, and each day Corrie ushered them into the warmth of their home. Betsie would wait on them, Father would comfort and talk with them, and Corrie would find a safe place out of Haarlem for them to go

The Ten Booms were helping a lot of people, but Corrie could see a few problems with their current plan. For one, the Beje was right in the center of town and only a block from the German secret police headquarters! Wouldn't the Gestapo notice all the people who came into the house? There was also the problem of how to feed all the hungry new mouths, since Jews could not get ration cards. Because of the war, many families did not have enough food even for themselves. Without ration cards for the hiding Jews, there would never be enough food for them. For this reason, safe houses, or places outside of Haarlem where the Jews could hide, were getting harder to find.

Danger was everywhere. The Gestapo could catch Corrie, Betsie, and Father hiding Jews at any moment, now that so many people came to them for help. As the house filled up with needy people, Corrie's fears only grew. *If the Germans found out, what would they do to these poor people? Where would they take them?* Corrie could not let that happen. *I must do all I can to help everyone who needs it!*

Once more, a thought occurred to Corrie. *Your Jesus is able to take care of this and much, much more.* How could she forget that? Maybe Corrie did not know where the help would come from, but God did! As Corrie said a prayer of thanksgiving, she decided to trust that God would provide exactly what they needed to get the job done.

To Corrie's delight, the Lord did provide! When they needed ration cards, God provided Corrie with an extra hundred cards through a friend. God also used the watch shop as a great way to hide Jews and help them move on to safety. Because the shop had a lot of business, Corrie could easily get people into her house without the Gestapo seeing. Corrie's nephew, Peter, also came up with clever codes to talk about hiding Jews.

Ration cards.

"Don't say, 'I have two Jews that need a place to hide.'" Peter explained, "Say this instead: 'I have two watches that need to be sent away.' Then, if someone overhears you talking, it will just sound like you're talking about the shop!"

Peter's idea was perfect. Now, other people like the Ten Booms who wanted to help the Jews could use the watch shop's secret codes too. Corrie was amazed. It seemed that there was always someone there to help, just at the very moment they needed it.

There was still one big problem. With so many Jews passing through the home, the Gestapo was sure to investigate the Beje soon. What would Corrie do if the Germans showed up at the door and demanded to come inside? Even though Corrie tried very hard to make sure everyone was safe, this truth always loomed in the back of her mind. Once again, she prayed earnestly for an answer.

Just as with all her other needs, the Lord provided an answer. One night, a family friend, a kind man that Betsie and Corrie had nicknamed Pickwick, knocked on the alley door.

"There are some people you have to meet," he told her. With that, he took Corrie to a home in a wealthy area outside of Haarlem. Waiting for her in a back room, away from the prying eyes of the secret police, were the members of the **Dutch Resistance**. These were people just like Corrie who secretly helped Jews. It seemed God had a whole army of people, right there in Haarlem, all doing their best to help. Urged on by Pickwick, Corrie told her story of hiding Haarlem's Jews and helping them to safety. She finished by explaining her greatest fear: that the Germans would find her Jews and take them away.

These people listened with sympathy, offering whatever services they could to Corrie's little operation. Pickwick directed Corrie to a man in the far corner.

"I hear your headquarters lacks a secret room," said the man. "I can help you with that."

Chapter

6

∞ Ambush! ∞

"Where are you hiding your nine Jews?" Waking up, Corrie rubbed her eyes. It was the summer of 1943, a couple months after the secret meeting with Pickwick. The bright beam of a flashlight shined directly at her face. She looked around groggily. Several shadowy figures stood around her bed in the dark.

"Nine? We only have six Jews."

"Oh, no, it can't be that bad!" one of the figures said.

Out of the shadow, Corrie's nephew, Kik, came forward. He was her brother Willem's youngest son. Kik shook his head and placed a hand on Corrie's shoulder.

"I know you're trying Aunt Corrie, but you have to try harder! Say, 'What Jews? We don't have any Jews here!'"

"Ugghh!" Corrie groaned, frustration creeping into her voice. "Can I try again?"

"Not tonight," Kik answered. "You're too awake. Practice more, and we'll have another drill on another evening."

Kik and the others left Corrie's room. She cradled her head in her hands, wondering how she could ever do what the others were asking of her. How could she keep the truth from the Germans? For one thing, Corrie was an honest person. She had been taught all her life that she should always tell the truth. But these Germans . . . they would take the truth and use it to kill her friends. Besides, Corrie answered to a higher authority—she must obey God by keeping her friends safe. It was not an easy thing, but Corrie chose to use her words to protect the innocent. Now, she just had to figure out how!

At least she could thank God that this was just a practice. If the soldiers had really come that night to question her, everyone in the house would have been in a lot of trouble. How could she keep her friends safe if she gave them away? *It should be simple!* Corrie thought. But it was so hard! Corrie would have to keep practicing. After all, her friends' lives depended on it.

Since the secret meeting with Pickwick and the Dutch Resistance, so much had changed in the Beje. The man whom Corrie had talked to in the corner went by "Mr. Smit." He had come by just as promised to inspect the house. After knocking on all the walls and investigating every nook and cranny of the old

Some of the Jews and resistance workers secretly hidden in the Ten Boom house.

rambling house, Mr. Smit gave Corrie the good news.

"This is a perfect house to build a secret room!" Mr. Smit declared with delight.

He chose Corrie's own bedroom, the highest point in the house. Within days, he got to work on it.

After he finished, Corrie could hardly believe her eyes. Her bedroom looked just as it had before. Was there really a secret room behind the wall? Mr. Smit excitedly gave her a tour, showing her the sliding panel that would allow people to get inside safely. Now, up to six people would be able to hide in the Beje if necessary.

Corrie's room, where the hiding place was built.

"The Gestapo could search for a year," he said proudly. "But they will never find this room!"

Of course, there was still a small problem. How would they know when the Germans were coming for a raid? Pickwick had an alarm system installed in the house so that everyone could be warned of any trouble. Corrie's nephew Kik took the lead on preparing them for raids. At random times during the day and night, someone would press the button on the buzzer system. Whenever the buzzer sounded, everyone had a job to do. The Jewish guests would take everything they had and get into the hiding place, leaving no trace behind. Father and Betsie would hide anything that looked suspicious. Corrie timed them, since all of this had to be done in under a minute. As everyone got better at hiding quickly, Kik focused more on helping Corrie prepare for when the police would ask her questions.

After their first practice raid in the night, Corrie realized just how hard it was going to be. The drills kept coming, and Corrie kept getting it wrong.

"Don't worry, Aunt Corrie." Kik said. "You're getting much better!"

At least, Corrie thought, everyone was getting the practice they needed! Kik's insistence on the drills helped everyone to get into the hiding place in time. Corrie also got better at answering questions. Even an older Jewish woman named Mary, whose asthma made it difficult for her to move or breathe, got into the hiding place quickly enough. Still, Corrie was nervous. She knew it was only a matter of time before the real raid would come.

"Corrie," Betsie said, gently shaking her awake. "There's a man downstairs asking for you. He said he would only talk to you."

Corrie sat up weakly, her head spinning. Nine months had passed since the secret room was built. It was now February of 1944. Corrie had been fighting the flu for a few days. Even with extra rest, she did not feel any better. Her head spun harder at the idea of talking with anyone right now, but Corrie knew it could be important.

A stranger asked to speak to Corrie.

Coughing and stumbling with the effort, Corrie went slowly along the handrail to meet the man. Corrie took a deep breath and opened the door. The stranger peered through the doorframe, speaking hastily as it creaked open.

"Miss Ten Boom! I need your help! The Gestapo took my wife! Our lives are in danger, and I hear you help Jews . . ."

Corrie's head throbbed as she tried to focus.

"I don't know how I can help," she answered, bleary-eyed. This was very strange. She did not know this man, and no one told her he was coming. How could she be sure he was telling the truth?

"Please, there's no time! All I need is money for a bribe to get her out."

Corrie hesitated again, not sure what to make of the man. Something seemed off, but she could not place a finger on it. He wasn't using any secret codes, either. But what if she was wrong? What if he really did need her help?

"I'll do what I can. Come back later," she finally answered.

"Thank you," he said, looking into her eyes for the first time. "I won't forget this."

Corrie closed the door and shuffled back up the stairs to bed. Worries crowded her mind as she drifted off into a fevered sleep.

Later that day, the sound of the buzzer jolted Corrie awake. She groaned, her head pounding with the sound. She sat up. Eusie, one of their Jews in hiding, sped past, his face white and his hands shaking. *What was happening?* Others ran past her bed too, ducking in behind the sliding panel of the secret room. Corrie gasped as she finally understood. *This was no drill!*

Six people disappeared behind the sliding door. Corrie slammed it shut as heavy footsteps crashed up the stairs. She quickly jumped back in her bed just as the bedroom door flew open.

A tall, large man, wearing a Gestapo uniform burst into the room.

"Your name!" he demanded as she lifted her aching head slowly from the pillow.

"Cornelia ten Boom," she replied, trying to sound sleepy.

"Ah! So you're the ringleader! Come on! Down the stairs!"

The man, a secret police captain, pushed Corrie ahead of him as she stumbled down the steps to the dining room. Father and Betsie sat in the room quietly. Other secret police agents were watching them with stern, cold eyes.

"Where are the Jews?" the captain shouted.

"Jews?" Corrie replied. "There aren't any Jews here."

He slapped her hard across the face, causing Corrie to fall to the floor.

"Jesus, help us!" Corrie cried as he hit her again and again. Still, Corrie did not give anything away. Silently she prayed, *Lord, keep our guests safe in the secret room!*

"If you won't talk," the man finally said, frustrated, "the skinny one will!"

He dragged Betsie to the next room. By now, the sounds of hammer blows and cracking wood echoed throughout the house as the other agents searched for Corrie's Jews. Corrie held her breath, praying they would not find the secret room. When the captain returned with Betsie, she was bleeding.

"Oh, Betsie!" Corrie said as Betsie collapsed beside her. Betsie looked at the man —not with hatred, but with pity.

"I feel so sorry for him," she said.

"Prisoners will remain silent!" he shouted, but his face had gone deathly white. And with that, he turned away, leaving Betsie, Corrie, and Father in the hands of the other Gestapo agents.

All the while, at the very top of the Beje, in the secret place in Corrie's room, the six hideaways crouched silently in fear. The same question played over and over again in each of their minds: *How did the Germans know?*

Chapter

7

❧ **Alone in Scheveningen** ❧

A tiny beam of light danced across the page of Corrie's palm-sized Bible as she read it silently, hanging on to every word. Her cell at the prison could be lonely, but every day she was thankful for God's grace in allowing her this one small comfort. She leaned against the hard, grimy wall, her own body and clothes just as dirty. Still sick and weak from the flu, she coughed violently.

It had been several weeks since the raid at the Beje, but Corrie remembered it as if it was yesterday. She remembered how they waited anxiously for hours as the Gestapo tore apart the house, smashing walls and steps and cupboards in search of the Jews they knew Corrie was hiding there. As each blow splintered through the walls, the Ten Booms prayed for their friends hiding in the secret room. After a long time, when the Gestapo still had not found anything, they took Corrie, Betsie, and Father to the police station. There they waited even longer. Finally, the Germans herded them outside, loaded them on buses and took them away.

It was then that Corrie recalled her vision. It was the one that came to her long ago, showing her that one day she and her loved ones would be taken away from home. *But where were they going?*

They found out two hours later, when the buses rolled to a stop outside of **Scheveningen** Prison. The Gestapo agents pushed them off the buses, put them into lines, and asked them endless questions. Father was in front of Corrie. He still look dignified despite all that had happened.

"Does that old man really need to be here?" said the chief agent as his gaze fell upon Father. He waved Father toward him.

"I can send you home, old man," he said, "as long as you give me your word you will not cause any more trouble."

Father stood tall as his bright blue eyes met the eyes of the agent. Finally, he shook his head. "If I go home today, I will continue to help as many as I can."

"Get back in line!" the chief agent growled angrily. "Now!"

When the processing was over, the guards separated the men from the women.

"Father!" Corrie cried. "God be with you!"

"And with you, my daughters," he replied. It was the last time Corrie would see her father.

Since no two people from Haarlem were allowed to share a cell, the guards took Betsie away from Corrie too. Without her beloved sister, Corrie was sent to live in a cramped cell with four other women. Eventually, because she was still so sick, the guards moved Corrie to a cell all by herself. Here Corrie waited, each day lonelier than the last.

Fighting fear and despair, she held tightly to her little Bible and read it every day. The Bible was a precious gift from a kind nurse in a hospital nearby. Since some prisoners, like Corrie, got too sick in prison, the guards had nurses and doctors check them. When the nurse asked Corrie how she could help, Corrie asked for a Bible. *And then God provided*, Corrie remembered. *It was a miraculous gift from Him!* She looked at the Bible lovingly. It was her only light in this dark, dreadful place.

Footsteps echoed down the corridor outside Corrie's cell door. Quickly, she hid her Bible in the folds of her dress, but no one entered. Instead, the metal flap where food came in flipped open. A letter slipped through it.

"A letter!" Corrie cried. "At last! Oh thank You, Lord!"

She hurried toward it and picked up the letter eagerly. It was a letter from Nollie, her older sister.

"This is strange . . . " Corrie said to herself as

she examined the letter. All of the writing on the envelope slanted toward the stamp. Curious, Corrie peeled the stamp away. There was a message in tiny, neat handwriting beneath: "All the watches in your closet are safe."

Corrie's heart soared as she wept happy tears. The message Nollie placed under the stamp was a code—the "watches" were the Jews hiding at the Beje. Everyone in the hiding place had escaped!

With a smile on her face, Corrie opened the letter.

"Father is free . . . " she read, her smile suddenly disappearing, " . . . of any more sorrow. He is resting in his Lord whom he loved so dearly."

Now the tears fell freely down Corrie's cheek once more and splashed onto the letter in her shaking hands. After all they had done, Father had not survived. It was so hard to understand why God would let this happen! And why did Corrie have to find out here, alone in a cold, dark prison?

"Oh, Lord," she whispered, her heart aching. "Help me to trust You . . . "

Suddenly, a thought came to Corrie: Father was safe now! *He was not suffering in a cold prison. He truly was free.*

She turned to the wall, where she had been marking her days in prison. At the bottom, she scratched the date into the cement: March 9, 1944. Next to it, she wrote: "Father. Released."

Even if Corrie did not understand God's plan right now, she knew He had one. Father was gone, but he was now with Jesus. That was the place he had been longing to be all of his life. Corrie cradled the Bible in her arms, thinking on these things as she drifted off to sleep.

Chapter

8

❧ Into the Pit ❧

orrie blinked in the bright summer sunlight as she stepped outside for the first time in months. It was now June 1944, and hundreds of other women stood with her, shading their eyes as they waited on the train platform. It had all been so sudden. One moment, Corrie was sitting in her lonely cell. The next, voices shouted at her to collect her things and get out as soon as possible. A long train puffed up to the platform and rumbled to a stop. As soon as the doors opened, the guards herded the women aboard like cattle.

A familiar head of pinned-back chestnut brown hair bobbed among the crowd. Could it be? Yes! It was Betsie! Corrie pushed her way through the masses.

In time, she wriggled in beside her dear sister. She reached out and squeezed Betsie's hand just as they were being pushed into the train car.

"Corrie!" Betsie shouted happily. Corrie hugged her tightly, crying. Though weak and awfully thin, Betsie hugged her too, tears streaming down her own face.

More and more women tumbled in after Betsie and Corrie until they could hardly move. The door slammed shut, leaving them in darkness. Corrie barely noticed, though, as she held firmly to Betsie's hand. Finally, they were together again! They spent the time telling their stories of the past few months. In time, the idling train rumbled to life and rolled forward.

"Where do you think they are taking us?" Betsie wondered aloud.

"I don't know," Corrie replied. "But at least we're together!"

A long time passed before the train stopped at a **concentration camp** called **Vught**, far southeast of the prison. Corrie hoped they would be released since there were whispers that the war was ending. Instead, the guards pushed the exhausted women out of the train and made them march for miles. When they finally got to the camp, Corrie's heart sank.

The dirty camp cut across the landscape like an ugly scar. Barbed-wire fences shut them in on all sides, leaving no hope for escape. The buildings were gray and rotting in the foul mud. Corrie passed piles of old, smelly straw that were crawling with lice. Harsh guards eyed them hatefully, shouting and pushing the women whenever they had the chance. In her heart, Corrie knew that this camp was meant to work and starve the prisoners to death.

Scared, Corrie squeezed Betsie's hand and hugged her little Bible close to her body. Amazingly, the guards did not search her and take God's Word away. How thankful she was that she could keep both Betsie and her Bible close! Even now, God had not forgotten about Corrie ten Boom.

And so, Corrie held on to hope. Every day, the sound of explosions came closer. There was talk that the Germans were losing the war. Could it be that they would soon be free? These thoughts of uncertainty filled her mind. Betsie, on the other hand, spent her time looking for every chance to show God's love to others.

"Oh, Corrie!" she would say, "Is there a better way to spend our lives? If people can be taught to hate, they can be taught to love! We must find a way, no matter how long it takes!"

Betsie amazed Corrie as she showed this kindness and love excitedly. Using Corrie's smuggled Bible, the two sisters taught the women in the camp about Jesus and the joy that could be found in Him.

But it was hard for Corrie. Vught was a joyless place. So many evils happened here. To make matters worse, Corrie learned who had betrayed her family to the Germans. It was Jan Vogel, the same man who had come to the Beje asking for bribe money before the raid. He was a spy all along, and Corrie hated him for what he did.

"You must forgive him, Corrie," Betsie urged her, "just as God forgives."

This, too, was hard for Corrie. And yet, Betsie forgave and even loved the man. She prayed for him even as she prayed with the women in their barracks, never missing an opportunity to talk about God's love. How strange were Betsie's great strength, joy, and love in the midst of so much sadness, bitterness, and pain! Corrie thanked God every day for her sister and prayed that she, too, would find a way to love and forgive. On the days when Corrie wanted to give up all hope, it was Betsie who kept her going.

Days turned into months as Corrie and Betsie survived at Vught. In late August of 1944, news came that help in the war effort was coming. Now, the countries fighting against the Germans included the United States, Great Britain, and the free Dutch forces. The entire camp was on edge as the guards rounded them up for roll call. Suddenly, in the quiet, gunshots rang out from the men's camp nearby. It went on for hours.

"This is no work camp!" a voice cried as the women wept around Corrie. "It is a death camp!"

"Move!" the guards yelled at the women, as they pushed them outside the tall fences of the camp. Terror gripped Corrie as they marched away. Too weak to walk the distance, Betsie stumbled along as Corrie half-carried her. Thankfully, they were met not with rifles but with train cars. The remaining male prisoners were already inside the cars. Once more Betsie and Corrie were stuffed inside an empty car with many other women. The train rolled forward. News came to them in whispers as it went along.

"We're going east!" someone said. "They're taking us to Germany!"

Germany.

Chapter

9

∾ The Fleas ∾

"Augh! Fleas!" Corrie wailed. "Betsie, how can we live in such a place?"

Corrie slapped at her leg as she tried to settle in their bunk, which was little more than a platform made of wood and stacked against the wall of the crowded barracks. It was now several days since the guards at Vught packed Corrie and Betsie into the train. The ride was a nightmare. Women were crushed against one another with no food, water, or clean air for three full days, only to be marched straight out of the cars for miles. Weak, tired, and covered in their own filth, the women nearly collapsed as they reached **Ravensbrück**, a death camp in dreaded Germany in September 1944.

Still very weak, Betsie leaned heavily on Corrie as they walked. They moved slowly through the dirty, dank camp. Corrie's heart was heavy. She knew it would be worse here than at Vught. Finally, Corrie and Betsie reached their assigned barracks. As they entered the room, they gasped at the terrible conditions that faced them.

Tired, sunken-eyed women looked out at them from the crowded wooden bunks—were these their beds? The room smelled of human waste and death. And what was worse, the whole place was covered in fleas! Though they could barely squeeze in, Corrie and Betsie wiggled onto the closest wooden plank. The women already lying there cursed and shuffled irritably at their arrival. Corrie could not blame them—on the inside, she was grumbling too.

And now, days later, Corrie's problem with these fleas was only getting worse. Betsie, however, seemed completely unaffected. As Corrie swatted and muttered under her breath, Betsie closed her eyes in prayer. Suddenly, Betsie's eyes snapped open and lit up excitedly.

"We shall thank God!" she said. "Don't you see? He's given us the answer—in 1 Thessalonians this morning, remember? Read that part again!"

Corrie paused her scratching to take the Bible out of her pouch. This was now her third prison, and for the third time, the Bible miraculously made it past the guards without being discovered.

"Comfort the frightened, help the weak, be patient with everyone. See that none of you repays evil for evil, but always seek to do good to one another and to all . . . "

"Go on! That wasn't all," said Betsie.

Corrie sighed heavily and scratched her leg before continuing. "Rejoice always, pray constantly, give thanks in all circumstances, for this is the will of God in Christ Jesus—"

"Yes! That's it!" Betsie exclaimed. "Let's start giving thanks right now for everything here!"

"For what?" Corrie sighed again, now scratching even harder than before.

"For this: Thank You, Lord, that we are here together," started Betsie. "And for what we're holding in our hands."

"Oh . . . right," Corrie said. "Thank You that we have Your Word, that there was no inspection to take it away, and that no guards have taken it. Thank You for all the women here, who are already meeting You in these pages."

"Yes," Betsie continued. "Thank You for the crowding here, so that so many more will hear! And thank You that Father is in heaven with You, and for the fleas—"

"The fleas!" Corrie exclaimed. "You can't expect me to be grateful for fleas!"

"It says to give thanks in all circumstances, Corrie." Betsie stressed. "Not just perfect ones. Fleas are a part of this place God put us and a part of His plan!"

65

"Oh, alright!" Corrie grumbled. "Thank You for these . . . fleas."

"Amen!" Betsie finished, smiling. "Isn't that better?"

Corrie turned away. Despite being so weak and sick, Betsie glowed, lighting up the ugly barracks around her. Even so, Corrie was sure she was wrong. How could she give thanks for these awful fleas, for all their pain, and for this terrible place?

It was now November of 1944, nine months since the ambush at the Beje and two months since their arrival at Ravensbrück. The bite of the winter air blew sharply across the muddy grounds as Corrie and Betsie moved piles of heavy dirt around the inside of the camp wall. It was hard, back-breaking work for Corrie, but for Betsie, it was impossible. Sick and weak, she could barely even carry her shovel, let alone move any dirt with it.

Noticing the tiny piles on Betsie's shovel, a female guard ripped the shovel from Betsie's frail hands.

"Look at this!" the guard taunted. "How pitiful! What makes you so special to barely lift a finger?"

The other guards laughed as they mocked Betsie, but to Corrie's surprise, she laughed too.

"Yes, that's me! But let me keep working with my little spoonful, or I'll have to stop altogether."

The guard's face twisted in anger as she hit poor Betsie.

"No!" Corrie cried, running toward Betsie with her own shovel ready to strike a blow. But Betsie caught Corrie's eye before she could reach them.

"Please, Corrie, stop! Look only at Jesus!" she pleaded. "Forgive!"

Forgive? Corrie blinked as her eyes welled up with tears. How could she forgive this? These guards, with their needless hate, could beat Betsie to death without batting an eye! And Betsie wanted her to *forgive* them? No, not that. It was too much to forgive.

"Please, Corrie . . ."

Corrie let her shovel fall to the ground. *For you, Betsie,* she thought. *Never for them.* Still shaking with anger, Corrie watched as the guard released Betsie with a final shove. *Never for them,* she thought again.

Betsie leads Bible study in the concentration camp.

For the next few days, Betsie led the Bible study. Corrie listened quietly as Betsie taught the good news about Jesus. The women hung on to her every word, hungry to hear more about this Jesus who loved them and longed to be with them. It did not matter where Betsie was—in the barracks, at work, in the sick bay, or the food line—she overflowed with talk about her great God. Corrie was astonished. Weak and abused as she was, Betsie was as bold as a lion when she spoke of her Savior.

After one such Bible study in the barracks, Betsie pulled Corrie aside.

"Corrie," Betsie whispered. "I have something extraordinary to tell you! Do you know why we've never been bothered here by the guards?"

Corrie thought for a moment. It was strange that the guards never came into their barracks. In fact, this was what allowed them to so freely pray and teach the Bible every day.

"It's the fleas, Corrie!" she said triumphantly. "They won't come in because they are afraid of the fleas!"

It was then that Corrie understood. Something so much bigger than all the evil of this war was happening here. As a tear trickled down her cheek, she bowed her head and truly thanked God for the fleas.

Chapter

10

⚶ Betsie's Vision ⚶

Betsie coughed weakly as she lay sick in the camp's hospital, blood trickling out of the corner of her mouth. It was a week and a half before Christmas, and Betsie was now so sick that she was unable to move. Corrie stood by her side, holding back tears.

But Betsie, eyes bright and full of wonder, seemed to forget her sickness and even the horrible camp that caused it. Grabbing Corrie's shirtsleeve, she whispered excitedly.

"There will be so much work to do. We will tell people what happened here, and they will listen! The Lord has shown me! There will be a house . . . a house with lovely wood floors, flowerboxes, great, tall windows . . . painted green, like springtime. A house where everyone who has been broken by this war can go to find God's healing. Oh, Corrie, can't you see it? We will be released soon, before the year is over!"

"We'll do this together, right?" Corrie asked. "You and me together after the war, right, Betsie?"

But Betsie did not answer. She was asleep. Corrie stood by Betsie's bed, tears splashing over her cheeks.

"I need you, Betsie," Corrie whispered softly, but the impatient attending nurse yanked on Corrie's arm.

"Time's up," the nurse said gruffly.

Corrie walked back to the barracks slowly with Betsie's words replaying in her mind. It was already the middle of December! Would they really be released before the year was over?

———◇———

Corrie prayed constantly for her sick sister, but Betsie looked weaker and paler with every passing hour. Every time she visited, Corrie thought of Betsie's vision of the house where people would come for healing. *Why didn't God heal her sister now if they were supposed to be released, as Betsie had said? What about all the work they were going to do?*

But something told Corrie this sickness would not pass. Worried and tired of waiting for news, Corrie snuck over to the hospital and peered into the window on December 16, 1944. Corrie gasped at what she saw. Inside, two nurses wrapped a sheet around Betsie's unmoving body and took her away. She was . . . dead? The nurses carried Betsie to a small washroom behind the hospital. Corrie hurried to the back of the building, tears stinging her eyes.

One of the nurses was waiting there at the door, but she did not scold Corrie. She just stepped aside quietly, watching as Corrie sank to the floor beside Betsie's body.

"Oh no, Lord Jesus! Please, no!" Corrie cried. "I can't do this without her!"

It was then that Corrie noticed Betsie's face, peaceful and content, as if she had fallen asleep. All the marks of this awful death camp—the sickness, pain, and hunger—were gone. She looked healthy and happy, as in the days before the war. Corrie gazed wonderingly at this, the realization dawning upon her. She had not lost Betsie, Corrie finally understood. Betsie was safe in the arms of the Lord.

New strength filled Corrie as she returned to her barracks. Sharing Betsie's story with the women there, she explained with joy that Betsie truly was free of Ravensbrück and resting now with Jesus. Many of the women listening trusted Jesus as their Savior too. Even in death, Betsie's love for God still brought hope to others.

A week after Betsie's death, other news began to rumble through Ravensbrück. The war was ending, and the Germans were losing. Corrie could see the fear in the eyes of her guards as they shouted and pushed the prisoners around. Corrie knew that they killed off the oldest and the sickest of the prisoners in their horrible gas chambers. Now, with defeat on its way, the Germans did not want anyone who had seen their crimes left alive. Even healthy prisoners disappeared every day.

On one of these days, Corrie stood outside during roll call. A voice boomed over the loudspeaker, calling a group of prisoners to the front.

"Cornelia ten Boom!"

Corrie whispered encouragement to the scared faces around her, reminding them to trust in Jesus. She followed the line of prisoners who shuffled away from the main group, ready for whatever lay ahead of her.

The guards took the prisoners to another part of the camp, where they all waited anxiously. Corrie noticed a young girl in line with her, teeth chattering with cold and fear. *This might be the last time I can tell someone about Jesus,* Corrie thought. She said a quick prayer for God's help, love, and wisdom.

"What's your name?" Corrie whispered to the girl.

"They call me Tiny," said the girl. "I've been here for two years."

"Have you ever read the Bible?"

"No," Tiny said softly, "But I believe God exists. I

wish I knew more about Him. Do you know Him?"

"Yes, I do—and I will tell you all I know," Corrie said. With the time she and Tiny had left, Corrie shared the good news about Jesus. Tiny listened to every word.

"Will you let Him into your heart?" Corrie asked.

"Yes," said Tiny, smiling.

What joy Corrie felt, even though she waited for death! She praised God as the group now moved forward. Suddenly, however, a guard pulled Corrie out of the line.

"This way," the guard said, shoving Corrie toward a different building.

Confused, Corrie followed the guard to a desk inside, where a paper was stamped and given to her, along with her old belongings. In stunned silence, Corrie read CERTIFICATE OF DISCHARGE in big, black letters across the top.

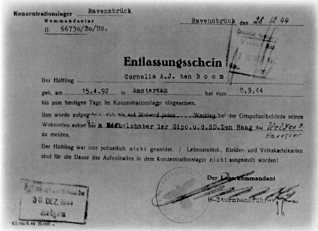

Corrie's release papers.

"I'm . . . free?" she asked in disbelief.

"Yes, now get out!" the guard said gruffly, casting her an annoyed glance. "Unless you want to go back in!"

"What day is it?" Corrie asked timidly.

"December 28," came the reply.

She walked out into the weak sunlight in a daze, each step taking her farther away from Ravensbrück. It was just as Betsie foretold. Before the end of 1944, both of them had been set free.

Corrie leaves the prison.

Chapter
11

A World Torn, A Great Mission

It all started with a paperwork error. The day that Corrie was scheduled for the gas chamber, someone made a small mistake on her papers. All it took was one wrong stamp, and everything changed. On that Thursday after Christmas, Corrie ten Boom walked free. Stunned that she was still alive, she left Ravensbrück and made her way through war-torn Germany. Finally she arrived in Holland and then home to the battered Beje in Haarlem.

Corrie was sure of one thing: *Betsie had been right.* There was so much work to do. Corrie grieved for the people of Haarlem. So many were homeless, the city's disabled were uncared for, and every home felt the painful impact of war. Corrie quickly went to work. With the help of her sister Nollie, who was still in Haarlem, she opened up the Beje to serve the needy people of the city. As in the days when the Red Cap Club bounded through the halls, the old house was once more open to those in need.

When the war ended, the German army left Holland, and Corrie saw the need grow even greater. The Dutch who survived the death camps of the Nazis returned to Holland, their hearts and bodies broken. There were also those Dutch citizens who had sided with the Germans. When the German occupation ended, the rest of the country turned on them with bitter vengeance. They were homeless, jobless, and hopeless. Yet, because of Betsie, Corrie knew that God's love was for all people. Corrie set out to help them in the only way she knew—by telling all about God's forgiveness.

For this reason, Corrie shared her and Betsie's story. She traveled far and wide, telling everyone hurt and broken by the war about God's great plan for healing. She spoke of His love and desire to save them and of the forgiveness that could only be found in His son, Jesus. Corrie talked too of Betsie's vision—of a peaceful home where the healing could really begin.

After one of these messages, a wealthy woman came up to Corrie.

"I think I can help you with Betsie's vision," she said. "I want to give you my old home to do this work. Let me show you."

Corrie went with the woman, her jaw dropping

Betsie's vision for a home of healing was fulfilled.

when she saw the house. It was the exact home Betsie had described— down to the flowerboxes in the windows and the green paint that looked and felt like springtime. For the first time, Corrie understood that everything Betsie had said was true. This was where God meant for the work to continue.

The home was opened, and in time, it was used to help people on both sides of the war to heal. God's plan was even more amazing than Corrie could imagine!

One day Corrie opened her mail to find a letter stamped by the country that had caused so much pain and suffering. A church in Germany was asking her to come and share her story there. Corrie clutched the letter tightly. *Could I really go back to the place where so much evil has happened? Am I able to face the pain of returning to so many terrible memories?* Though she dreaded it, Corrie felt God's tug on her heart once more. She knew the German people needed to hear about God's forgiveness and healing as much as those who suffered at their hands.

And so in 1947, three years after her release from Ravensbrück, Corrie stood before a crowded German church. The silent audience watched her anxiously as she prepared to speak.

"When we confess our sins," she said, "God casts them into the deepest ocean. They are gone forever!"

Shock and disbelief registered on their faces. Many of these people once actively supported the Nazi leaders who used the war to do so many evil things. Corrie could see the questions in their minds: was it true? Would God forgive even the worst of their sins? Corrie bowed her head. *Lord, thank You for leading me back here. How these people need to know of Your love and forgiveness!*

When she finished bringing her message of hope, the silent crowd left, all except for a man in a gray coat. He came forward timidly, tears in his eyes and a look of shame on his face.

Corrie's blood froze. This was not just any man. This was a man whose face she knew. He was a guard from Ravensbrück, one who caused so many to suffer. Corrie recalled how cruel he was there. He beat the prisoners—even her own sister—without mercy. The man reached out his hand to shake hers, but Corrie's hand lay limply at her side.

"You must know me, since I was a guard at Ravensbrück, though I don't remember you," he said, still holding his hand out to her. "I know God has forgiven me for what I have done. As you have taught us, our sins are no more. But, I would like to know that you forgive me too."

With his face twisted in pain and regret, the man continued to reach for Corrie's hand.

"Will you forgive me?" he asked.

For what seemed like an eternity Corrie stood there, finally coming face to face with the most difficult decision of her life. She knew what he said was true—that God did forgive all things if one asked—but could she now forgive this man, who did not even remember her? Could she forgive *him*,

Corrie forgives a former Nazi guard.

who heartlessly beat starving women and watched without pity as Betsie slowly died?

Her emotions told her to turn away and to hate him for all he had done. She knew she could never want to forgive this man. Yet, she also knew that God had forgiven her—over and over again, even though she did not deserve it. Forgiveness was not an emotion. It was something that her heavenly Father could grant her if she only asked.

Help me, Lord, she whispered in her heart. *Help me to want to forgive.*

Corrie lifted her hand and slowly grasped the fingers of the man before her. Suddenly, warmth flooded her heart. It filled her until it sprang forth in a wave of tears. She could feel God's intense love and joy in their handshake as He healed both of their broken hearts.

"I forgive you!" she cried. "I forgive you from my heart."

As they cried together, Corrie finally understood what God's forgiveness meant. Hatred, bitterness, and sorrow could no longer hold onto her and keep her trapped in the pain the war had brought. She was able to love just as her Jesus loved her. And, just like this guard, she was now truly free.

Corrie ten Boom never ceased to give testimony to Christ and to tell her story all around the world.

Epilogue

The German occupation was a dark time for Holland. Three-quarters of Holland's Jews died in camps during the war. Many other citizens paid the same price for trying to save them.

Casper ten Boom lived for two weeks after the German raid on his house before dying in Scheveningen Prison on March 9, 1944. He was eighty-four. Betsie was fifty-nine years old when she died at Ravensbrück on December 16, 1944. Due to a clerical error, Corrie was released before the year was over on December 28, 1944. Willem, Nollie, Peter, and Kik were also arrested and sent to prison. Only Corrie, Betsie, and Kik were sent to the concentration camps. Willem, Nollie, and Peter were granted release before Corrie and Betsie were sent to Vught.

However, Willem's prison stay was not without consequences. Tuberculosis contracted in prison caused his death at age sixty in December of 1946. His son, Kik, also paid the ultimate price, dying at Bergen-Belsen camp in 1945. Peter survived the war and dedicated his life to serving God with music. He, his wife, and five children formed a singing group that shared God's message of love throughout Europe and the Middle East.

After the war, Corrie visited sixty-four countries in twenty years. Her story touched and changed the lives of millions of people. She also wrote many books to share God's love with the world. All the days of her life, Corrie never stopped talking about the love of Jesus and the forgiveness of sins that could be found in Him. Corrie ten Boom died on her ninety-first birthday, April 15, 1983.

The Ten Boom family gave everything, and the world remembers them for their love, sacrifice, and obedience to God. Today, their legacy lives on in the Beje, which has been converted into the Ten Boom Museum. For more information, visit the official website at www.corrietenboom.com. To enjoy a virtual tour of the museum, please visit www.tenboom.org.

ᴥ **Bibliography** ᴥ

Benge, Janet and Geoff Benge. Corrie ten Boom: *Keeper of the Angel's Den*. Seattle: YWAM Publishing, 1999.

Smith, Emily S. *More Than A Hiding Place*. Haarlem, The Netherlands: The Corrie ten Boom House Foundation, 2010.

Ten Boom, Corrie. "I'm Still Learning to Forgive." Guideposts, 1972.

Ten Boom, Corrie and C. C. Carlson. *In My Father's House*. Old Tappan, New Jersey: Fleming H. Revell Company, 1976.

Ten Boom, Corrie and Jamie Buckingham. *Tramp for the Lord*. New York: Berkley Books, 2002.

Ten Boom, Corrie, Elizabeth Sherrill, and John Sherrill. *The Hiding Place*. Grand Rapids, Michigan: Chosen Books, 2006.

❧ Timeline ❧

1892 - Cornelia Arnolda Johanna (Corrie) is born April 15, Good Friday, to Casper and Cornelia ten Boom.

1897 - Corrie is five years old when her family moves into the house above the Ten Boom Watch Shop at Barteljorisstraat nineteen. The house becomes known as "the Beje." Corrie prays and gives her life to Jesus this year.

1910 - At 18 years old and a year out of high school, Corrie begins Bible school in Haarlem. The Ten Booms hold a mission study group in their house.

1914 - World War I begins.

1918 - Mama has a major stroke. World War I ends, and the Ten Booms take in a family from Germany.

1920 - Corrie is 28 when she completes her watchmaking apprenticeship in Switzerland.

1921 - Mama dies on October 17. Corrie (29) begins working in the watch shop full time.

1925 - Corrie is 33 when the Ten Booms take in needy children of missionary families. The seven foster children become known as the Red Cap Club. Corrie also starts various other Christian girls' clubs and works with them until 1940.

1937 - 100th anniversary party of the Ten Boom Watch Shop. Corrie is 45.

1940 - Nazis invade Holland beginning May 10.

1942 - Corrie (50) decides she must save Jewish people and becomes involved in the underground resistance to the Nazi government.

1943 - The Ten Boom family takes many Jews and underground workers into their home to hide. Through the underground movement, Corrie helps to find safe places out of the city to send the people.

June 2: The secret room, or "hiding place," is built in Corrie's top floor bedroom; the family and their guests begin holding drills to practice for raids.

1944 - On February 28, while Corrie is sick in bed, the Gestapo raids the Beje around 5:00 p.m. At 11:00 p.m., Corrie (52) and her family are arrested.

February 29: Corrie and her family are sent to Scheveningen prison in Holland.

March 1: After hiding for two days, all the people in the

hiding place are rescued by other underground workers.

March 9: Father ten Boom dies in a Nazi prison at age 84.

March 16: Corrie is sent to a prison cell by herself because of her sickness. While there, Corrie receives news that all the people in the hiding place are safe.

June 5: Corrie and Betsie are sent by train to Vught Concentration Camp in Holland, along with many other prisoners. They arrive June 6 and stay for three months.

September 4: Corrie and Betsie spend three awful days crammed into the boxcar of a train with other prisoners. They are taken to Ravensbrück Concentration Camp in Berlin, Germany.

December 16: At 59 years old, Betsie dies at Ravensbrück Camp after sharing a vision with Corrie. Her vision is of Corrie's release and of a large peaceful home where people can heal after the war.

December 28: Corrie is released.

1945 - On January 1, Corrie is 52 when she makes her way back to Holland and finds her brother, Willem.

May 5: Holland is liberated from German occupation. Corrie begins sharing her story and Betsie's vision.

Touched by the story, a wealthy woman donates a home like the one Betsie had seen in her vision to help war victims.

May 8: World War II ends in Europe.

1946 - Corrie travels the world with her story. On December 13, her brother, Willem, dies from an illness he contracted while in prison. He is 60.

1947 - Just two years after the war, Corrie returns to Germany. She meets a guard from Ravensbrück and forgives him.

1948–1979 - Corrie continues to travel the world. She writes several books, including *The Hiding Place,* during this time.

1975 - *The Hiding Place,* a film based on Corrie's book, premieres in September.

1983 - After suffering a series of strokes, Corrie dies on her birthday, April 15. She is 91.

❧ Glossary ❧

Adolf Hitler – The leader of the Nazi party and of Germany.

Beje – Pronounced "bay-yay," this is the nickname of Corrie's childhood home above the Ten Boom Watch Shop. This home becomes the Ten Booms' base for helping others during the German occupation of Holland.

Concentration camp – A place where the prisoners of the Nazis were sent to work as slaves. Conditions in concentration camps were so bad that the prisoners would often die from starvation, sickness, or cold. Those who survived all of this were sometimes killed, or "exterminated," by the Nazis.

Dutch – Common name for the people of Holland and the language they speak.

Dutch Resistance – A group of Dutch people who secretly rebelled against the Germans and their occupation of Holland. The Dutch Resistance helped save the Jews from the Nazis. Because they worked in secret, they were known as the "Underground."

Gestapo – The Nazi secret police who enforced Nazi rules during the occupation of Holland.

The National Socialist Bond – A group of Dutch people who supported the ideas of the Nazi party.

Nazis (or the Nazi party) – A group of people from Germany who believed that white people were better than others. They also believed that other kinds of people, like Jews and the disabled, were worthless and caused many of the world's problems. They thought that getting rid of the Jews and the disabled would make a better world.

Holland (The Netherlands) – The country in Europe where Corrie lived. It is north of Belgium and west of Germany. Its official name is the Kingdom of the Netherlands, but is often called by the name of its largest territory, "Holland."

Ravensbrück – A concentration camp in Germany that was known for being especially harsh and cruel to prisoners.

Scheveningen – A village in the west of the Netherlands and location of a well-known prison.

Vught – A village in the south of the Netherlands and location of a concentration camp.

Now you can watch the amazing true life stories of heroes of the faith!

THE TORCHLIGHTERS
HEROES OF THE FAITH
The Corrie ten Boom Story

An amazing story of courage, sacrifice, and forgiveness

THE TORCHLIGHTERS
HEROES OF THE FAITH
The Eric Liddell Story

THE TORCHLIGHTER
HEROES OF THE FAITH
The Jim Elliot Story

His ultimate sacrifice lit a torch that could not be extinguished

THE TORCHLIGHTERS

An animated DVD series that recounts the courage and dedication of people who made a difference!

Each episode contains an engaging animated adventure and a full-length documentary all with English and Spanish audio tracks.

Jim Elliot	**Perpetua**
William Tyndale	**Amy Carmichael**
John Bunyan	**William Booth**
Eric Liddell	**Samuel Morris**
Gladys Aylward	**Corrie ten Boom**
Richard Wurmbrand	**John Wesley**
	… with more in the works!

Be a Torchlighter and light up the world!

Visit **www.torchlighters.org** to watch previews.
Order your copies today at www.visionvideo.com
or by calling 800-523-0226